Supporting Children with
Epilepsy

Hull Learning Services

David Fulton Publishers

David Fulton Publishers Ltd
The Chiswick Centre, 414 Chiswick High Road, London W4 5TF

www.fultonpublishers.co.uk

First published in Great Britain by Hull Learning Services.

David Fulton Publishers is a division of Granada Learning Limited, part of ITV plc.

Copyright © David Fulton Publishers 2004

British Library Cataloguing in Publication Data
A catalogue record for this book is available from the British Library.

ISBN 1 84312 223 5

Typeset by Matrix Creative, Wokingham
Printed and bound in Great Britain

Contents

Foreword

This booklet was written in partnership with the Educational Service for Physical Disability (ESPD), the Special Educational Needs Support Service (SENSS) and the Specialist Paediatric Epilepsy Nurse.

It is one of a series of eleven titles providing an up-to-date overview of special educational needs for SENCOs, teachers and other professionals, and parents.

The books were produced in response to training and information needs, raised by teachers, support staff and parents in Hull. The aim of these books is to raise awareness and address many of the issues involved in creating inclusive environments.

This is not a definitive set of guidelines, but rather draws on the experiences and up-to-date knowledge of those whose position it is to take a lead in this area. As such this overview will add to this knowledge in supporting children with epilepsy.

We would like to thank senior adviser John Hill for his support and encouragement throughout the development of this series.

For details of other titles and how to order, please see page 52.

In the production of this booklet the following have acted as representatives of services within Kingston upon Hull. Appreciation is given to the time and effort given to its publication.

Lesley Kynman: Education Service for Physical Disability
Chris Morley: Specialist Paediatric Epilepsy Nurse
Elizabeth Morling: Special Educational Needs Support Service

Introduction

A minority of pupils with epilepsy are educated in special schools; however, for the most part pupils with this condition attend mainstream schools and have access to the full curriculum with minor adaptations or modifications, if necessary.

Up to eighty per cent of pupils with epilepsy have seizures which are controlled by medication. This book should help schools in the development of management plans for those pupils whose epilepsy is not under medical control; raise awareness of the possible educational implications; and suggest strategies to overcome difficulties.

Inclusion rights

The SEN Code of Practice (DfES November 2001) states that '... the Special Educational Needs and Disability Act (2001) amends the Disability Discrimination Act (1995) to prohibit all schools from discriminating against disabled children in their admissions arrangements ...'

- Epilepsy is covered by the Disability Discrimination Act (2001).
- Therefore all pupils with epilepsy have a right to an education in their local mainstream school.

To support inclusion the Act recommends that:

- Schools should make reasonable adjustments to accommodate pupils with SEN so they are not disadvantaged by their condition.
- This may involve restructuring policies and practices so they can respond to the educational implications of the pupils' learning needs.
- Schools should also look at curriculum delivery, especially the way written information is presented, to make it more accessible to pupils with learning needs.

The 'Index for Inclusion' points out that diversity of the school population should not be viewed as a problem to overcome, but as a resource to support the learning of all, since inclusion in education is simply one aspect of inclusion in society.

Please see Appendix 3: Legal framework, for more information regarding meeting the legal requirements for pupils with epilepsy.

Definition and causes

Epilepsy is defined as *'a condition in which there is a tendency for a person to experience recurring epileptic seizures over a period of time'* (Walker & Shorvon). Seizures are a symptom of the condition, and the type of seizure experienced indicates the area of the brain affected.

Epilepsy is in reality a group of syndromes (over 40 have been identified) having different symptoms, resulting from different causes, with different prognoses, and requiring differing treatments.

It is therefore more accurate to talk about 'epilepsies' in the plural; however, in this document we use the term 'epilepsy' to cover *all* the different conditions.

Causes

The trace produced by an electroencephalogram (EEG) machine is the result of continuous electrical activity within the brain. As long as this activity operates below a certain 'threshold' there is no problem; however, a sudden burst of excessive electrical activity within the brain which goes *above* this threshold would result in a seizure.

Whether an individual develops epilepsy depends on two factors, their inherited threshold level, and life circumstances. Any of the causes below would come under the heading of 'life circumstances':

- brain damage due to a difficult birth;
- a severe blow to the head;
- a stroke which starves the brain of oxygen;
- blood chemical abnormalities, e.g. low calcium, magnesium or glucose;
- an infection of the brain such as meningitis;
- very rarely, a brain tumour.

Epilepsy resulting from any one of these is called **'symptomatic (or secondary) epilepsy'** since it is a symptom of the primary condition or infection.

However, in as many as 6 out of 10 cases there is no clear identifiable cause for the epilepsy. This is termed **'idiopathic (or primary) epilepsy'**. Into this group would fall those with an inherited low seizure threshold.

Some facts

- Depending on the source, epilepsy affects between 1 in 133 and 1 in 200 of the UK population – although the incidence in children is higher; possibly as high as 1 in 100.

- It is the second most common neurological condition after migraine.

- A single seizure does not normally indicate that a person has epilepsy (1 in 20 individuals will experience a single seizure at some time in their lifetime).

- It can affect anyone regardless of age, sex, ethnic origin or intelligence; however, it most commonly develops before the age of twenty.

- Every day about 81 people in the UK will be told that they have epilepsy.

- In most instances epilepsy can be controlled by medication.

- Many children with childhood epilepsy will grow out of it.

- The terms 'petit mal' and 'grand mal' have been replaced by more descriptive names of the seizures involved.

- Referring to someone as being 'epileptic' is no longer considered to be appropriate, 'a person who has epilepsy' would be the preferred terminology.

- Likewise 'fit' is no longer used, 'seizure' being preferred and more descriptive.

> **The word 'epilepsy' comes from the Greek language and means 'to take hold of, or seize'.**

The brain, nerve cells and how they function

The brain is divided into two halves, with four lobes in each hemisphere. The left hemisphere controls the right side of the body and the right hemisphere controls the left side. Therefore damage or injury to one side of the brain affects the *opposite side* of the body.

Brain tissue is comprised of billions of nerve cells consisting of a body with dendrites radiating off, and a long arm (axon) with branches.

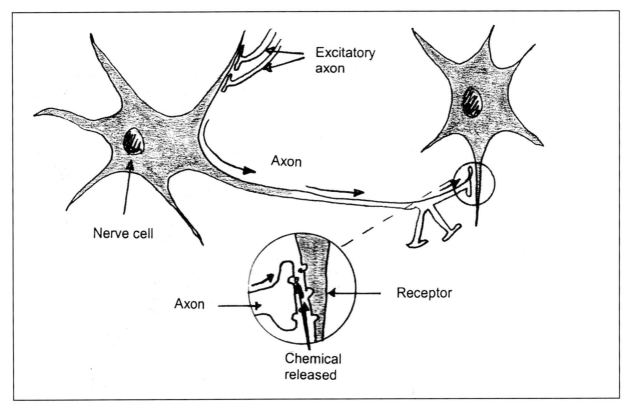

Diagrammatic representation of nerve cell and axon

Brain activity depends on the transmission of electrical signals. These signals pass along the long arm of the neuron like messages down a telephone line. If the level of the stimulus, i.e. 'excitation', of the nerve cell is sufficient it triggers a chemical carrier to be fired across the gap between the nerve cells.

However, if only excitation occurred in the brain all cells would fire at once creating an 'electrical storm', as seen in a seizure. There is also, therefore, a chemical inhibitor which only allows the strongest stimuli to pass from cell to cell.

During normal functioning there is a balance between these chemicals; however, if there is too much of either excitation or inhibition in part of the brain at any one time, a seizure would result.

This explains why the extremes of over excitement and boredom are potential triggers of seizures (see page 10 for more details).

Seizure types

Seizures fall into two groups –

- **generalised seizures** in which electrical activity occurs across the *whole* of the brain and during which consciousness is impaired;
- **partial seizures** which are restricted to only *part* of the brain (the 'focus', sometimes termed **'focal epilepsy'**) and during which consciousness may or may not be impaired.

N.B. These are not mutually exclusive, e.g. an episode may begin with a partial seizure which then becomes generalised across the whole of the brain (termed a 'secondary generalised seizure').

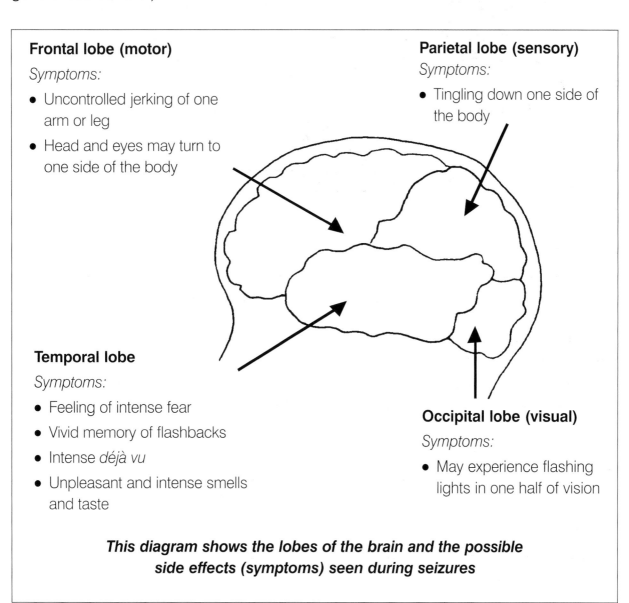

Frontal lobe (motor)

Symptoms:

- Uncontrolled jerking of one arm or leg
- Head and eyes may turn to one side of the body

Parietal lobe (sensory)

Symptoms:

- Tingling down one side of the body

Temporal lobe

Symptoms:

- Feeling of intense fear
- Vivid memory of flashbacks
- Intense *déjà vu*
- Unpleasant and intense smells and taste

Occipital lobe (visual)

Symptoms:

- May experience flashing lights in one half of vision

This diagram shows the lobes of the brain and the possible side effects (symptoms) seen during seizures

Childhood epilepsy

Childhood absence seizures (previously known as 'petit mal')

This is the most common form of childhood epilepsy. The pupil may look blank and stare, with possible twitching or blinking and a brief loss of consciousness lasting for a few seconds only. He/she may look pale but is able to continue normal activity almost immediately. N.B. Absence seizures can easily be mistaken for 'day dreaming'.

Action required:

- Record the time of day and frequency (to see if a pattern emerges) to pass on to parents/specialist.
- Reassure if necessary.
- Note possible information that the pupil may have missed since the cumulative effect of absence seizures on short term memory can significantly reduce academic progress.

Tonic-clonic (previously known as 'grand mal')

This is the classic seizure of which most people are aware. The pupil loses consciousness, falls to the ground (with possible injury) and becomes stiff (the 'tonic' phase). He/she may gasp as air is expelled from the lungs in the initial muscle spasm.

Upper limbs tend to be flexed and the pupil may hold his/her breath, becoming cyanosed. The 'clonic' phase consists of short, sharp jerks with alternate contraction and relaxation of muscles. Incontinence may occur.

Action required:

- Protect the pupil from injury by clearing the area around him/her and putting something soft underneath his/her head.
- Ensure airway is clear and stay with the pupil until the seizure has ended.
- *Do not* try to restrict movements or put anything in his/her mouth (see tonic-clonic response details in Appendix 6).
- Record time and frequency, possible information missed, and reassure pupil.
- Allow the pupil to recover at his/her own speed.
- Try to maintain the pupil's dignity at all times.

Both these seizures belong to the 'generalised seizure' group because the electrical activity is across the whole of the brain and there is loss of consciousness.

Benign Rolandic seizures (also known as 'simple partial seizures')

This affects about 10 – 15% of all children, with epilepsy usually starting between the ages of 4 and 10 years, and often stops at puberty (14–18 years).

The seizure is confined to one area of the brain and consciousness may or may not be lost. However, the symptoms experienced by the pupil will be dictated by the area of the brain affected (the focus).

The most common focal 'motor' seizure usually begins with a tingling (like pins and needles) affecting the tongue, face, lips and cheeks. Speech may be affected with accompanying twitching (clonic movements) or stiffness (tonic movements) of one side of the face. These movements may then spread to the arm and leg on the same side.

Focal 'sensory' seizures are very variable and may be emotionally disturbing for the pupil (see page 5 for possible symptoms).

Sometimes the seizure develops across the whole of the brain to become a secondary generalised seizure.

This form of epilepsy is not associated with learning difficulties.

Complex partial seizures

The pupil loses consciousness completely, or becomes vague, looks dazed and does not respond when spoken to.

Generally he/she does not fall but may carry out movements such as clapping hands, smacking lips, chewing, biting, etc. Plucking at, or the removal of clothing are also symptoms and occasionally aggressive behaviour occurs.

Seizures normally last 2–3 minutes followed by a period of confusion. They may be preceded by an **'aura'** or warning, usually sensory, e.g. visual, auditory or taste, etc.

N.B. In both these types of epilepsy the individual has no control over the seizure and is unable to stop or control the symptoms.

Action required for both of the above:

- Do not try to stop or restrain the pupil.
- Remove harmful objects and guide away from danger.
- Talk quietly and reassure the pupil if necessary.
- Record time, length of seizure and frequency, and possible information missed.

Atonic drop attacks (rare)

With this seizure there is a sudden loss of muscle tone and the pupil falls to the ground. Younger pupils with this type of epilepsy often wear a crash helmet to reduce injury.

Myoclonic seizures (also rare)

These are similar to atonic drop attacks but differ in that there is a sudden muscle 'jerk' after which the pupil falls to the ground. In both, consciousness is lost for a few seconds only and the pupil recovers quickly with no after effects, e.g. confusion or tiredness.

Action for both:

- Talk quietly, reassure the pupil and try to maintain dignity.
- Record time and frequency.
- Check for injury and treat if necessary.
- Staff will need to give careful consideration to safety issues for these pupils.

'Status epilepticus'

If a seizure lasts for *more than the usual length of time (approximately 5 – 10 minutes)* or if the pupil has *recurrent seizures one after another* follow the emergency strategy for 'status epilepticus' found in the pupil's Individual Health Care Plan (IHCP).

A convulsive seizure, i.e. a seizure involving alternate contraction and relaxation of muscles such as one sees in tonic-clonic epilepsy, is more serious than a non-convulsive seizure, e.g. complex partial epilepsy. Although less urgent, the latter would still require hospitalisation.

Emergency action:

- Initial response – as for seizure type.
- Ensure a member of staff stays with the pupil.
- Dial 999 for an ambulance and inform parents.
- If the seizure is convulsive the trained member of staff should administer rectal diazepam as soon as possible since this will reduce the severity and effect of the seizure.

What could be mistaken for epileptic seizures

Febrile convulsions

Only seen in Nursery/Reception pupils these seizures are *always* linked to high temperature and seen in association with childhood illness, e.g. tonsillitis or teething, etc.

They are most common between the ages of 12 months to four years and rarely seen over the age of five.

They usually involve tonic-clonic or clonic only movements lasting about two minutes.

> **Action required:**
> - Try to bring temperature down by sponging with tepid water.
> - If the seizure lasts longer than three minutes consult emergency procedure in the Individual Health Care Plan.
> - Record time and length of episode.

Syncope

This is the medical term for fainting and due to lack of oxygen to the brain. It may be in response to pain, standing for a long time in a hot place, shock, etc.

The usual sequence is, the person would become dizzy and then pale, and fall to the ground. As soon as this happens the blood normally returns to the brain and consciousness is quickly regained.

Migraine

Migraines can begin with visual disturbances and occasionally with tingling down one arm, symptoms which are similar to those experienced during a partial seizure. However, consciousness is never lost and the visual disturbances are distinctly different.

In most cases there is little doubt about whether the symptoms are caused by epilepsy or migraine.

Breath holding attacks (usually only seen in small children)

Children who do this turn blue only, but may occasionally pass out if strong willed. Attacks usually stop of their own accord.

Triggers of individual seizures

Forgotten or incorrect medication	• This emphasises the importance of keeping accurate records to pass on to the pupil's GP or specialist.
Illness / high temperature	• Any illness which results in an increase of temperature could result in a seizure. • Sunstroke would have the same effect. • In these situations it is important to lower the body's temperature by regular doses of paracetamol, and use a fan or sponge down, if necessary.
Lack of sleep or food	• Generally this falls within the province of the family; however, it does have implications for residential visits.

Emotional stress	• This would include bullying and teasing in the school situation, although other factors may be involved, e.g.
	   – worry about their condition;
	   – will they make/lose friends;
	   – can they take part in the same activities as the rest of their peer group, etc.

Excitement/boredom	• Note the extremes. It has been reported by school staff that pupils seldom have a seizure when they are focused on an activity.
Flashing lights	• Only 3–5% of people with epilepsy are in fact photosensitive. Very rarely a pupil may have 'reflex epilepsy' which has other sensory triggers, e.g. loud noises, music, touch, etc.
Changes in hormone levels	• Particularly noted prior to the menstrual cycle.
Drugs/alcohol	• All teenagers may be inclined to experiment with these as a way of expressing their individuality.

Diagnosis and treatment

The most important contribution towards a diagnosis of epilepsy comes from the 'medical history' provided by the family, e.g. whether there has been a head injury, illness, problems at birth, etc.

Eye witness accounts with detailed reports of seizures from parents and/or school also contribute to this. However, the following tests may need to be carried out:

EEG (electroencephalography)

This records electrical activity within the brain. The EEG trace of some individuals who have experienced seizures may show unusual patterns, e.g. spikes or spike/wave patterns. If these are seen it means that there is a 99% probability of their having epilepsy.

One particular EEG pattern called a *3 per second spike and wave* is seen in individuals with absence epilepsy. This is treated with a specific form of medication and the outcome is generally good.

MRI or CAT scans

These investigate the internal structures of the brain. *CAT scans (computerised axial tomography)* give pictures of 'slices' of the brain which show any abnormalities, e.g. brain haemorrhages, tumours, etc.

MRI scans (magnetic resonance imaging). These are gradually replacing CAT scans as normal practice since the pictures produced are much clearer and give greater detail.

Blood tests

Blood is tested to check general health and more specifically levels of calcium, magnesium and glucose (possible metabolic causes of seizures).

Long term treatment

Effective seizure control is gained in 75–80% of those with epilepsy by the following means:

1. Avoidance of all known seizure 'triggers'.
2. Medication* (correct dosage of certain drugs is monitored by regular blood tests and feedback from parents and school staff).
3. Brain surgery (very rare and only after lengthy tests are carried out).

* See Appendix 2 for commonly used medication and possible side effects.

Well known people with epilepsy

Politicians & Leaders

Julius Caesar
Napoleon
Alexander the Great
William III
Queen Boadicea
Alfred the Great
William Pitt

Saints

St Paul
Joan of Arc

Philosophers

Socrates
Aristotle

Composers & Musicians

Handel
Hector Berlioz
Paganini

Writers & Poets

Edward Lear
Dostoyevsky
Tennyson
Lord Byron
Guy de Maupassant
Edgar Allan Poe
Charles Dickens
Gustave Flaubert

Scientists & Mathematicians

Pythagoras
Isaac Newton
Alfred Nobel
Blaise Pascal

Films & the Media

Margaux Hemingway
Reginald Bosanquet
Bud Abbott
Claire Gorham

Sports & Athletes

Tony Greig & Jonty
Rhodes (Cricketers)
Doug Wert (Golfer)
Gary Howatt (Hockey)
Danny Glover (Rugby)

Artist

Van Gogh

It is apparent that individuals with epilepsy cover the whole range of intelligence and accomplishments. However, evidence suggests that a disproportionate number of pupils with epilepsy do not achieve well academically, which has implications for teachers and schools.

Educational implications

Since epilepsy affects individuals across the whole ability range there are bound to be some pupils with learning, language and communication, or behavioural difficulties. However, these may also occur for other reasons, especially if the epilepsy falls within the difficult to control range.

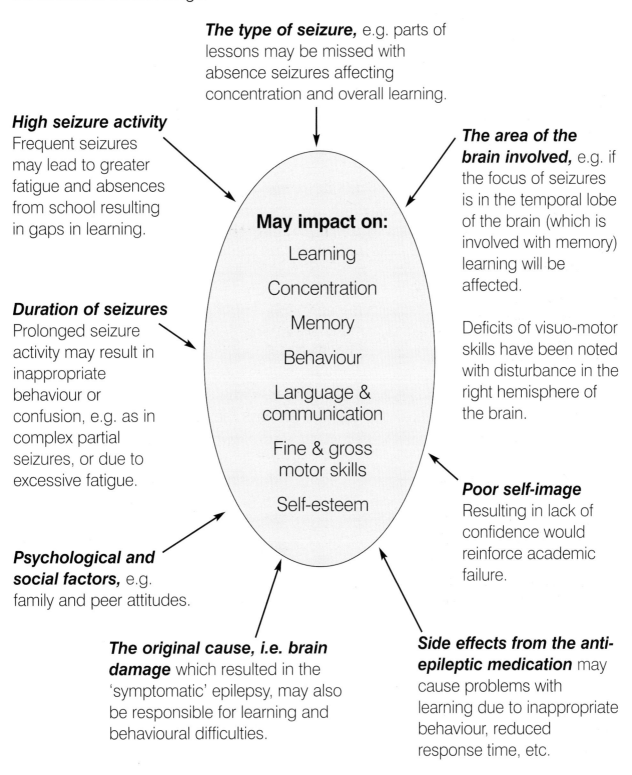

The type of seizure, e.g. parts of lessons may be missed with absence seizures affecting concentration and overall learning.

High seizure activity
Frequent seizures may lead to greater fatigue and absences from school resulting in gaps in learning.

The area of the brain involved, e.g. if the focus of seizures is in the temporal lobe of the brain (which is involved with memory) learning will be affected.

Deficits of visuo-motor skills have been noted with disturbance in the right hemisphere of the brain.

Duration of seizures
Prolonged seizure activity may result in inappropriate behaviour or confusion, e.g. as in complex partial seizures, or due to excessive fatigue.

May impact on:

Learning

Concentration

Memory

Behaviour

Language & communication

Fine & gross motor skills

Self-esteem

Poor self-image
Resulting in lack of confidence would reinforce academic failure.

Psychological and social factors, e.g. family and peer attitudes.

The original cause, i.e. brain damage which resulted in the 'symptomatic' epilepsy, may also be responsible for learning and behavioural difficulties.

Side effects from the anti-epileptic medication may cause problems with learning due to inappropriate behaviour, reduced response time, etc.

13

How memory might be affected

Short term memory

Dr Martin Wells states that short term memory is used for *specific tasks* relating to *present actions* and involves electrical activity.

Short term memory is therefore used to carry out given tasks or sets of instructions in the classroom and to move from one step to the next, i.e. to stay on task.

> **Implications for teaching:**
>
> - pupils with absence seizures will not only not hear instructions but the disruption to the electrical activity in the brain will also result in poor concentration and difficulty staying on task;
>
> - also if seizures last for more than three seconds it has been found that while the pupil's performance of simple tasks is not affected, their performance in more complex tasks is poor (Stores);
>
> - anti-epileptic medication may result in a 'dampening' effect on the brain activity with consequences for concentration and memory.

Long term memory

The process involved with long term memory is more complex and depends on the creation of links and associations to many other nerve cells (Buzan). Apparently a large single neuron is capable of making 10,000 or more possible connections.

Our knowledge of the world is gradually built up by the continuous stream of information received by the brain through our senses. The more senses involved in the process the more likely an event will be remembered, i.e. by creating new links and associations.

More complex skills, such as reading, are made up of many subsets of skills which are built up hierarchically. For these to be transferred effectively to the long term memory also depends on repetition and over learning.

> **Implications for teaching:**
>
> - the multi-sensory approach is more effective in helping the pupil to form links and associations (Stores);
>
> - any sensory or physical impairment due to underlying brain damage will result in faulty information being received by the brain;
>
> - disruptive electrical activity may impair the development of long term memory, therefore there may be gaps in learning resulting in specific difficulties.

How behaviour might be affected

- There is some concern that anti-epileptic medication causes difficulties with behaviour; however, evidence suggests that this is *not* the case.

- While it may be true that behaviour problems are more frequently observed in pupils with epilepsy, the reasons are not fully understood.

- Influential factors may include the stress of having unpredictable seizures, low self-esteem, or consciousness of feeling different to their peers.

- Sometimes medication *can* affect mood, making pupils depressed or hyperactive. This tends to be dose-related rather than the drug itself.

- Pupils with partial or focal seizures may demonstrate bizarre or repetitive behaviours as symptoms of the seizure. It is important that teachers recognise this and do not confuse it with physical or verbal aggression.

- Unacceptable behaviour within school must be treated in the same way as any other pupil, i.e. with firmness and consistency. N.B. Reprimanding a pupil will not bring on a seizure.

- Sometimes restrictions placed on pupils, particularly adolescents, can lead to anger and frustration. It is important to allow young adults to be part of the decision-making process and provide opportunities within school to promote independence.

Language and communication problems associated with epilepsy

- Seizures can cause dysfunction in one or more areas of the brain.

- If these areas are concerned with the understanding and organisation of language and communication, this will have a consequence for the pupil.

- Effects may vary from delayed or interrupted development of language skills to more specific problems, e.g. difficulties with word-finding, social communication, and slow or slurred speech.

- Some difficulties can be linked to a specific epilepsy syndrome, i.e. Landau-Klefner (detailed information relating to this can be found on the Epilepsy Action web site).

- Pupils with certain types of epilepsy may also have pragmatic difficulties such as poor turn-taking, excessive or restricted topic-maintenance, and poor communicative intentions, e.g. difficulties with questioning, greeting, seeking attention, describing and commenting.

- Pupils with absence seizures may experience problems with language acquisition and processing, which results in difficulties following general conversation.

- Some pupils may have very subtle language problems. This is particularly the case with the mainstream pupil who has no obvious learning difficulty but has a history of behavioural problems and/or difficulties relating to other people.

The role of the school

Put into context the incidence of in 100 of the UK childhood population having epilepsy means that in a medium sized primary school (300 on roll) 3 pupils will be affected, and in a large primary (600 on roll) 6 pupils will have the condition.

Every school should therefore be familiar with the condition of epilepsy and plan to meet the individual needs of each pupil. The Headteacher and Governing body should bear in mind the legal framework (Appendix 3) during planning.

Developing a Whole School Policy

- As with any area of the curriculum it is vital to have a whole school approach to meeting the needs of pupils with epilepsy.

- An example of a Whole School Policy which can be modified by individual schools to fit the format of existing policies within the school can be found in Appendix 4.

- It is usually the responsibility of the Special Needs Coordinator to draw up the policy under the guidance of the Headteacher. This should then be distributed to staff for comments before being ratified by the Governing body.

- A school policy will help staff to feel comfortable with the educational implications of epilepsy and ensure that parents are confident about a school's ability to meet their child's needs.

Raising awareness

The Headteacher should arrange in-service training (INSET) to:

- raise awareness of the condition;

- ensure seizure recognition and ability to describe the main symptoms;

- demonstrate correct management response for all seizures, especially generalised tonic-clonic seizure (see Appendix 6);

- recognise possible triggers;

- endorse the individual seizure response for each pupil with epilepsy in school;

- understand the possible educational implications of the condition.

Approach the Epilepsy Support Nurse, Paediatric Support Nurse, Schools Clinical Medical Officer or the Physical Disability Support Service to assist if the pupil falls within the 20–25% of those who have difficult to control epilepsy. See sample Staff INSET format in Appendix 5.

Nominating staff to administer drugs

- If drugs such as rectal diazepam need to be administered to a pupil during a seizure the Headteacher must ensure that written permission is obtained from the parents (see IHCP in Appendix 9). There are also training implications.
- Two or three members of staff would be required to volunteer to undertake training, e.g. a teacher, a class or child support assistant (CSA), a Lunchtime Supervisor, etc. and be prepared to administer the drug in an emergency.
- In reality the occasions when these drugs need to be administered are rare.

Training nominated staff

- Training can be arranged through the local Children's Centre/Paediatric Nurse or the pupil's GP.
- It usually involves watching a video, listening to a talk and possibly using a plastic model for training purposes.

N.B. Existing staff cannot be forced to undertake these duties, however when writing a job description and interviewing for support staff these duties should be outlined and an undertaking to carry them out sought prior to appointment.

Identifying an area for storage and administering of drugs

- Drugs should be clearly marked with the pupil's name and the required dosage.
- They should be stored in a secure, cool, dark place which is within easy reach of the pupil's classroom. A high shelf in a cool store room is usually sufficient, or the fridge in the staff room would be suitable if close by.
- Drugs usually need to be administered with some urgency; however, it is essential that it is done in a way that does not compromise the pupil's dignity.
- Medical advice is *not* to move any individual during a seizure regardless of the situation in which it occurs, unless the pupil is in danger.
- It will be necessary to calmly remove peers from the classroom or area in which the seizure has taken place (such an arrangement would need to be written into the pupil's Individual Health Care Plan).
- Always ensure that rectal diazepam is administered with a witness of the same sex as the pupil in attendance if possible.

N.B. It is anticipated that emergency medication will be delivered by oral spray in the near future. This will significantly improve the situation.

Record keeping

- Accurate record keeping is essential in assisting the medical profession to monitor the pupil's condition.

- Record keeping can also chart the effectiveness of drug changes.

- A communication system should be set up between the parents and/or the support nurse to ensure good information gathering and that records reach the appropriate agencies (see Appendices 7 and 8 for sample proformas).

Information sharing

- Consider how information will be shared with staff and others who work with the pupil.

- Some schools use an *'Alert Card'* system – a card with the pupil's name, class and a current photograph together with a photocopy of tonic-clonic seizure response (Appendix 6) placed in the school office/staff room/Head's Office.

- Be aware of issues of confidentiality when displaying such information.

Writing an Individual Health Care Plan (IHCP)

This forms an integral part of the pupil's IEP and will cover all the main points mentioned above, as follows:

- the names of those responsible for carrying out the emergency medical procedure;

- as precisely as possible the circumstances in which it would be carried out, and where;

- what is required (materials, facilities, knowledge, etc.);

- where medication is stored, etc.;

- who is the line manager/contact person in emergencies;

- the routine for the replenishment of stocks of materials/medication;

- the procedure to be followed if named staff are absent.

The IHCP should be written in conjunction with parents who should sign it and receive their own copy (Appendix 9). Parents are responsible for informing the school of any changes either in medication or the nature of the pupil's seizures which will affect the IHCP.

'At risk' factors

A risk assessment may need to be carried out in certain situations to ensure the safety of both the pupil and staff.

School organisational issues

Anti-epileptic medication gives 75–80% of pupils the opportunity to lead normal lives. However, the following considerations apply to the remaining 20–25% of pupils:

New staff	Ensure that all new staff are made aware of the school policy and have undergone basic training by watching the tonic-clonic seizure response video (made by staff during INSET day on epilepsy training) and additional training if necessary.
Timetable implications	Timetable lessons on the ground floor if possible for safety reasons (see Legal framework Appendix 3).
Safety issues in lessons	Certain subjects, namely Science, Food Technology, PE and some elements of Art, will have safety issues. Staff will need to consider the following:
• Science	Use of protective clothing, e.g. aprons, goggles, gloves as appropriate. Effective use of test tube racks and clamps, etc. How support workers will be used, balancing the need for safety with the need for independence, identify: 1. which activities the pupil can do without support; 2. division of task, with the support worker completing any activity considered to be a danger and allowing the pupil to complete the remaining part of the task; 3. activities which need to be completed by the support worker due to safety issues but under the pupil's direction.
• Food Technology	Fit a pan guard to a cooker hob. Encourage the pupil to use the back hot plate/burners. Teach microwave cooking techniques. Ensure the pupil does not carry hot pans (take plates to the cooker instead).

• **PE**	PE should be assessed on an individual basis according to the Individual Health Care Plan. Contact sports, e.g. rugby, hockey and football, should be safe if normal safety measures are taken. It may not be advisable to play contact sports if the epilepsy was originally a consequence of head injury.
Movement around school	Assess the need for adult supervision during movement between classes or break times. Ideally this should be distance supervision to encourage independence. Consider putting a 'buddy' system in place. Consider 'drop off points' in locations around school to reduce the number of books carried at any one time.
Peer group support	The pupil's peers should have some understanding of their fellow pupil's condition in order to be supportive. If necessary they can alert school staff to changes in the pupil's condition (be sensitive to the pupil or parent's wishes).
Development of life skills	Encourage the pupil to develop a whole life ethos which should help to reduce the incidence and consequences of his/her seizures by: 1. keeping stress to a minimum – teach coping strategies in conjunction with parents; 2. learning to pace himself/herself; 3. allowing time for rest and play; 4. taking regular exercise and eating healthily; 5. having regular counselling sessions (if necessary); 6. asking for staff support to develop strategies to deal with teasing or bullying; 7. taking part in out of school hobbies/activities.

The role of the teacher

Teachers can make school a positive experience by supporting the pupil in the following ways:

- be a positive role model for the other pupils by responding in a confident, calm and positive manner to the pupil with epilepsy;
- treat the pupil exactly the same as the others in the class and give appropriate responses, which should help to normalise the condition;
- avoid regarding the pupil's condition as an illness;
- also avoid letting him/her use epilepsy as an excuse;
- help to develop the pupil's confidence and encourage him/her to deal with new or difficult situations;
- accept that the pupil may feel angry and resentful about the condition at times;
- be aware of the pupil's seizure type, the Individual Health Care Plan and where medication is stored;
- monitor and record changes in behaviour, mood and performance, as well as physical stamina, academic achievement and social interaction since this may help in the review of medication.

Classroom management

- provide a pupil friendly environment;
- ensure the pupil is always in clear view (not sitting with his/her back to the teacher) so that any changes mentioned above can be noted;
- aid organisational skills by clearly labelling drawers or colour coding areas, etc,;
- provide somewhere quiet to sit with a friend, e.g. a book area or library, etc. after a seizure has occurred or if he/she feels unwell (N.B. always ensure that he/she is within an adult's view);
- ensure that key words and main points are included in classroom displays for each topic/module.

Teaching style

The multi-sensory approach illustrated below is an effective and proven teaching style to use with pupils who have problems with learning and/or memory. If possible try to ensure that as many of these strategies are included in each learning module.

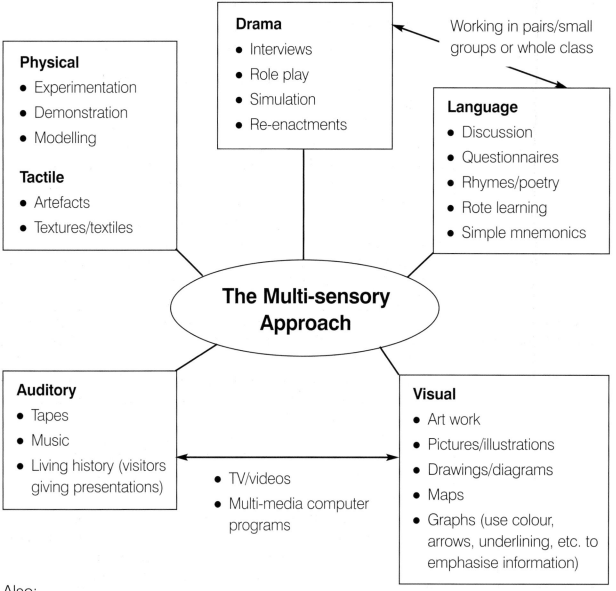

Also:

- plan systematic revision of work covered;

- pre-teach new vocabulary (use word webs to link concepts);

- give opportunities for new work/skills to be used in different situations to encourage transfer of knowledge;

- always use age appropriate written or spoken language and adjust to the ability level of the pupil if necessary;

- provide multiple choice answers to questions to reduce reliance on memory;

- visual and auditory elements in each module can be sent home with pupils overnight/at the weekend, etc. to reinforce the subject, or fill in missed areas of learning.

Classroom strategies

Concerns about:	Try the following:
Behaviour	• be firm, set clear boundaries for behaviour and state consequences of actions; • give simple and concise instructions with visual clues if necessary; • be consistent in expectations – the pupil is part of the group and has to conform; • ensure all staff are aware of strategies being used (reinforcement) and involve parents wherever possible; • try to ignore bad behaviour and comment on good behaviour only – use star charts, five minutes working on the computer, visits to the Headteacher, etc. as rewards; • expect compliance – give instruction and say 'Thank you'; • if no progress is seen consult the school's educational psychologist, or refer to a clinical psychologist, for advice. Some LEAs have a behavioural outreach service which provides support for teachers in mainstream schools.
Language & communication	• report any difficulties to the SENCO who should seek parental permission to refer to a speech and language therapist for an assessment; • if a speech and language therapy programme is already in place try to integrate as many aspects as possible into daily classroom interaction; • always ensure that you have the pupil's attention and that he/she makes eye contact during the conversation/discussion; • check that the pupil has understood instructions through sensitive questioning; • for problems in the area of social communication try to structure situations in which the pupil can practise a specific skill; • when planning work give as many opportunities as possible for the pupil to use language meaningfully.
Short term memory/poor concentration	• provide visual clues, e.g. photographs/objects of reference; • make 'cue' cards – pictorial for younger pupils and presented either singly for each step, or as the full sequence; • use 'post its', e.g. to develop organisational skills; • put key words/ideas on the board; • provide the parents with vocabulary for the next teaching module so it can be practised prior to starting work; • highlight important points in notes; • make visual timetables.

Long term memory	• revisit work done on a regular basis;
	• teach the pupil how to make effective notes – concise, under numbered points and with key words underlined/highlighted;
	• help the pupil plan his/her revision;
	• produce 'mind maps' for each module to give the pupil an overview of the work covered.
Tiredness/lethargy	• ensure that parents have passed on information regarding nocturnal seizures (home/school book);
	• note problem and possible learning missed;
	• keep a record to pass to consultant/parent;
	• provide differentiated work if appropriate;
	• ask parents to send in high energy slow release snacks, e.g. bananas/dried fruit for breaks, to maintain energy levels;
	• ensure that the pupil has a regular intake of fluids.
Photosensitivity	• for the 3–5% of those who fall into this group care will need to be taken when using computers, e.g. fit a glare screen if necessary, take regular breaks away from the screen (Health & Safety Guidelines), etc.;
	• sit the pupil in the shade in a sunny classroom;
	• ensure he/she wears sunglasses outside on bright sunny days.
Watching TV	• seat the pupil well away from the screen (more than 2.5 metres is the recommended distance) and at an oblique angle;
	• ensure that the room is well lit.
Video games	• similarly take frequent breaks and play in a well lit room;
	• avoid playing if the pupil is tired;
	• stop if dizziness, blurred vision, loss of awareness or twitching occurs.
Specific learning difficulties with reading/writing	• ask the SENCO to refer the pupil to SENSS;
	• try to improve self-confidence since this increases motivation;
	• make work achievable – set 'small step' objectives and praise success;
	• find out what the pupil's strengths are and try to teach to these.
Physical disabilities, visual/hearing impairment	• refer to the relevant support service for advice.
Visual perception/ handwriting difficulties	• use a multi-sensory method of teaching writing involving tactile activities, hand/eye coordination, whole body movement and language, etc.;
	• use a visuo-perceptual writing programme, e.g. 'Write from the Start' available from LDA;
	• teach cursive script from the beginning rather than print since the hand learns whole word patterns and fluency is developed much earlier (this is less effective with pupils with a learning delay since they are often unable to work out where the letter starts and ends);
	• if no progress is made refer to a paediatric occupational therapist for an assessment (this is initiated by a parental request through the GP).

Use of support staff

Pupils whose epilepsy is not under medical control will require some level of additional adult support to cover the following areas:

Appropriate seizure response

- Support staff would need to be trained to respond appropriately when a seizure occurs in accordance with the Individual Health Care Plan.

Safety issues

- Adult support may be required in subjects where safety issues are involved, namely:
  - Science
  - Food Technology
  - PE
  - Art (some aspects).
- Teaching staff will need to decide how the support is used (see page 19).

On-site mobility

- Support staff may need to be present as pupils move around the school site. Distance supervision allows the pupil as much independence as possible.

Educational support

- Additional learning, speech and language programmes, and measures to support behaviour issues may be required.
- The support worker would deliver programmes devised by the teacher and/or the relevant support service.

Monitoring seizure control

- Support staff can monitor progress and seizure control especially during changes in medication.

Developing personal skills

- Support staff can play a key part in promoting independence, confidence and self-esteem.

Out-of-school activities

Allow pupils with epilepsy to participate in the same activities as their peers unless medical advice is to the contrary.

The following issues need to be considered during planning:

School visits

Pupils should be included in school visits given adequate supervision. However:

- prior visits should be made to assess possible problems and contingency plans drawn up;
- medication should be taken (if appropriate) and the pupil's IHCP;
- a person trained to give emergency treatment should be included in the party;
- make up an emergency pack, e.g. mobile phone, a light cover to maintain the pupil's dignity during delivery of medication, contact numbers and the address of the local hospital.

Residential visits

As above but also:

- be aware that excitement and fatigue caused by lack of sleep may trigger a seizure;
- consideration should be given to maintaining stamina levels, e.g. on walks, by giving dried fruit, plenty of fluids, etc.

Swimming

Swimming should be encouraged and safety ensured by:

- informing a qualified life guard of the pupil's condition;
- adopting a 'buddy' system for all pupils which means that special attention need not be drawn to the pupil with epilepsy;
- ensuring the pupil is easily but sensitively identified, e.g. by wearing a coloured 'T' shirt;
- making sure that the pupil swims in the lane next to the edge;
- avoiding very busy pools.

N.B. If a seizure occurs while the pupil is in the water, support the head until the seizure ceases, help the pupil out of the water and continue the IHCP.

Water sports

This covers a wide variety of activities and guidance varies with the particular sport:

- sub aqua diving should be avoided;
- consult the British Sports Association for the Disabled for extra guidance (see Useful Contacts).

Discos and theatre visits

- Check the pupil's IHCP to see if they have photosensitivity (3–5% of epileptic pupils are photosensitive);
- be aware that seizures can be triggered by disco or theatre lighting.

Cycling

Where seizures are controlled there should be no extra risk. However:

- avoid busy traffic;
- if seizures still occur avoid public roads;
- ensure the pupil is always accompanied;
- cycle helmets should be worn at all times.

Horse riding

Similarly:

- normal hard hats should be worn;
- pupils should be accompanied;
- busy roads should be avoided.

Climbing and mountaineering

Heights can be a danger to people with epilepsy. However, the risk is small if seizures are well controlled and normal climbing safety guidelines are followed.

N.B. Safety plans should always be in place if this is undertaken.

Examinations and career options

Examinations

- Be aware that seizures may be triggered by fatigue or stress either approaching or during examinations.

- Inform the relevant Boards in advance of any pupil with epilepsy who may be sitting an exam.

- If a pupil has a seizure just prior to, or during, an exam inform the Board immediately.

- Absence seizures are more difficult to spot. If possible, sit the pupil close to a familiar member of staff acting as invigilator, who is more likely to recognise absences.

- Special arrangements can be requested if evidence is provided and depending on the pupil's needs, e.g.:

  i)   rest periods can be requested if fatigue is a major problem;

  ii)   if there are any subjects in which the pupil already has adult support for safety reasons, e.g. Food Technology, Science, etc. adult support can be requested for the examination;

  ii)   additional options, if the pupil has either a learning or a physical need, are 25% extra time, the use of a word processor if this is the pupil's usual method of recording work, and a reader and/or an amanuensis (look on the QCA web site for the latest guidance).

Career options for pupils with epilepsy

- For the 75–80% of individuals whose epilepsy is under medical control the range of career options will depend on aptitude and ability.

- Teaching and nursing are both open to pupils with epilepsy, with a few restrictions depending on the individual teacher training college.

- The only definite restrictions for this group are:

  - aircraft pilot
  - ambulance driver
  - merchant seaman
  - LGV, PCV or taxi driver
  - train driver
  - jobs in the armed services, fire brigade or police.

- Working with computers would also be an issue if photosensitivity has been noted as a trigger of seizures. Apart from this the usual Health & Safety Guidelines should be followed.

- Once a decision about the area of work has been made it might be wise to check with the governing body of that occupation to ensure that there are no specific restrictions. The details of the pupil's epilepsy would need to be at hand.

Specific advice

- For those whose epilepsy is more difficult to control (20–25%) career guidance would need to be offered on an individual basis.

- When choosing options in Year 9 teachers would need to be familiar with the pupil's academic abilities, social skills, the type and frequency of seizures, etc. to ensure that the pupil is advised correctly with regard to appropriate career paths, e.g. if seizures are not controlled pupils may not be employed in work at heights, near open water, or around unguarded machinery or fires.

- Any work involving driving would be restricted for this group of pupils.

- In Years 10 and 11 parents might like to pursue the possibility of either voluntary work or a local Saturday job on behalf of their son/daughter. This allows prospective employers to see the individual rather than the condition.

- Encouraging pupils to stay in further education as long as possible would give a clearer indication of strengths and ability as well as build confidence. Additionally many colleges now have ACCESS Centres who can provide an assessment for equipment or funding.

- The Employment Medical Advisory Service (EMAS) gives free advice about the suitability of particular jobs for pupils with epilepsy.

- Seek specialist advice from the Careers Service (Connexions), the UK Employment Service or the Disability Employment Advisor (DEA), as appropriate.

- Read the latest information regarding employment on the Epilepsy Action web site.

Emotional issues

Issues which may arise

Pupils with epilepsy have been reported as functioning below expectations on tests of social skills and social maturity. They appear to have fewer peer contacts and lower self-expectations. (Verduyn)

These quotes illustrate the feelings expressed by some pupils:

"My mum doesn't let me do anything in case I have a fit."

"My family and friends understand – I just wish other people would understand."

"I don't like having fits because I'm the only one who's got it at my house and my school."

"I never get invited to parties – mum says it's because other parents are afraid of me having a seizure."

They may also experience:

- verbal bullying or teasing;
- frustration caused by the restrictions that their condition may bring;
- fear of what is happening to them during the seizure or what their peers may think/feel;
- anxiety related to seizures occurring in a public place;
- (with younger pupils) the feeling that there is something 'wrong' with their brain or that they may die during a seizure – all due to the lack of understanding about the condition of epilepsy;
- teenagers may experience feelings of isolation – being a teenager means wanting to be like everyone else.

Strategies to support the pupil

Developing the pupil's confidence gives him/her a greater ability to assert himself/herself. Try the following:

- Discuss with parents whether there is a need to appoint an appropriate person to explain about his/her condition, e.g. the Epilepsy/Paediatric Support Nurse.

- Acknowledge that it is reasonable for the pupil to have feelings of resentment, anger, etc. and that it is acceptable for him/her to express these feelings.

- If required plan a brief weekly counselling session for the pupil with an assigned member of staff to discuss social and educational concerns.

- Involve pupils in decision making, e.g. when writing Individual Health Care Plans/IEPs, etc. from an early age.

- Develop structured activities at playtime to include isolated children (involve lunch time supervisory assistants), e.g. ring games, ball games, skipping games, etc. and encourage participation in lunch-time clubs.

- Use 'circle time' to allow issues to be raised and discussed.

- Use PHSE to educate other pupils about epilepsy with both the pupil's and the parents' permission (see Appendix 11 for some ideas).

- Use the 'Circles of Friends' book if you feel that social isolation is a serious concern.

- Encourage the pupil to be as independent as possible.

- Give the pupil the opportunity to participate in the same activities in and out of school as his/her peers (refer to IHCP to ensure this is appropriate).

- Ensure that bullying or teasing related to the pupil's condition is not tolerated.

- Install the Epilepsy Action and National Society for Epilepsy (NES) web sites on one of the school computers and encourage pupils to look up information for themselves:

  - Epilepsy Action has a Kids page (with various activities to do, and an email address if he/she would like to ask a question, etc.);

  - likewise for teenagers there is the opportunity to ask 'Debbie' or 'Danny' personal questions about worries or concerns, and fact sheets to download, etc.;

  - the NES web site has a message board for teenagers to chat to one another, a short quiz about epilepsy and a book list for reference.

- Some forms of complementary medicine have been found to be beneficial by promoting relaxation, thereby reducing stress, e.g. Yoga. If the pupil is interested consult with parents and check with the family GP.

Developing self-esteem

Pupils with epilepsy may have low self-esteem linked to achievement in school or emotional issues related to their condition. The following strategies may help to build confidence:

- ensure all staff are aware of the pupil's condition, Individual Health Care Plan, possible IEP and the implications of these;
- encourage the pupil to make contributions to his/her IHCP and IEP and to be a part of the review process;
- have a positive attitude to the pupil's condition;
- encourage the pupil to be open and share information about the condition with his/her friends, to enable them to offer support;
- older pupils should be encouraged to keep a diary noting the date of any seizures, time and severity plus any pertinent facts, e.g. late night out, etc. (this information helps the specialist as well as being a learning process in self-management for the pupil);
- the adult's manner should always convey to the group that the pupil is a valued member of the class;
- build on the pupil's strengths;
- reward success, academic or otherwise, with real congratulations and praise;
- make all goals attainable;
- display the pupil's work;
- celebrate the pupil's successes with his/her parents;
- give all pupils the same curriculum opportunities bearing in mind particular strategies noted in the Individual Health Care/Educational Plan;
- staff should share knowledge of the pupil as he/she makes any transition, e.g. at the end of each academic year, describing strategies which have been effective in supporting the pupil.

Home/School/Health liaison

For pupils with epilepsy to be fully supported in the mainstream environment there must be effective communication between the home, relevant health professionals and the school.

To create and maintain this relationship the following suggestions are made:

- The SENCO should gain as full a picture as possible about the pupil's epilepsy from the parents (see sample questionnaire in Appendix 7).
- Create an Individual Health Care Plan (see Appendix 9) for the pupil – involving parents, health professionals, school staff and the pupil (if appropriate).
- Information from the above should be disseminated to all school staff.
- Maintain a dialogue with parents, either verbally or through a home/school book (this should ensure school staff are aware of changes at home which may have implications in school, e.g. if a pupil has had an early morning or nocturnal seizure).
- School staff should, in turn, report any significant changes or occurrences which take place during the school day.
- Staff should be informed of any changes in medication and possible implications.
- Joint meetings may need to be arranged between health, school staff and parents to ensure effective management of the pupil's condition in school.
- Parents should be aware of the Code of Practice (CoP) and its implications for them – explain the three stages within the Code and let them know which stage their child is at.
- Invite parents and pupils to IEP planning meetings and reviews.
- Provide parents with reports before annual reviews in line with the CoP/LEA.
- Parents should know who to contact if they have concerns about their child through the following hierarchy:
    - Class teacher
    - SENCO
    - Headteacher
    - Special Needs Governor.
- Parental concerns should be listened to and acknowledged.
- Encourage parents to become involved in the life of the school.
- Inform parents of visits from other professionals, e.g. Educational Psychologist.

Further information

Epilepsy Action (formerly British Epilepsy Association)	Materials and web site at <www.epilepsy.org.uk>
'Understanding Epilepsy'	Dr M Walker & Professor S Shorvon BMA (Family Doctor Series) 1996
'Epilepsy Education in Schools'	Helen Coleman & Alison Fielder Paediatric Nursing Vol 11 No 9 November 1999
The David Lewis Centre	Handouts (see page 36 for address)
'Epilepsy & Education: A Medical Symposium on Changing Attitudes to Epilepsy in Education'	Various contributors (in particular Gregory Stores, Ronald Radley & Chrissie Verduyn) Education in Practice 1987
The National Society for Epilepsy	Handouts & web site at <www.epilepsynse.org.uk>
'The Educational Implications of Disability: A Guide for Teachers'	Judith Male & Claudia Thompson RADAR (The Royal Association for Disability and Rehabilitation) 1986
'Commonsense Methods for Children with Special Needs'	Peter Westwood Routledge 2003
'The Brain' (Chapter 5)	Dr Martin Woods BBC Publications 1969
'Circles of Friends'	Colin Newton & Derek Wilson Folens Publishers 1999
'Managing Medicines in Schools'	Joe Harvey Folens Publishers 1999
'Index for Inclusion'	Centre for Studies on Inclusive Education 2000

Books available for children:

'Illustrated Junior Encyclopaedia of Epilepsy'	R Appleton Pretroc Press 1996 ISBN 0948270608
'Lee the Rabbit with Epilepsy' *(The Special Needs Collection)*	Deborah M Moss Woodbine House 1989
'Edith Herself'	Ellen Howard Atheneum Press 1987
'Lefty Carmichael Has a Fit'	Don Trembath Orca Book Publishers 2000
'Becky the Brave'	L Lears & G Piazza Albert Whitman & Co 2002 ISBN 080750601X

Suggested reading for parents:

'Understanding Epilepsy'	Dr M Walker & Professor S Shorvon BMA (Family Doctor Series) 1996
'Your Child's Epilepsy: A Parent's Guide'	R Appleton, B Chappell & M Beirne Class Publishing 1997 ISBN 1872362613
'Epilepsy: Practical and Easy to Follow Advice (Your Child)'	F Marshall Vega Books 2002 ISBN 1843332760
'The Facts about Epilepsy'	C Llewellyn Belitha Press 2001 ISBN 080750601X

Useful contacts

Contact a Family (CaF) Directory of Specific Conditions and Rare Syndromes
020 7383 3555

Epilepsy Action (formerly British Epilepsy Association)
Anstey House, 40 Hanover Square
Leeds L53 1BE
Helpline 0808 800 5050 or email helpline at <www.epilepsy.org.uk>

British Sports Association for the Disabled
020 7490 4919

David Lewis Centre
Alderley Edge, Mobberley
Cheshire SK9 7UD
0156 587 2613
<www.davidlewis.org.uk>

National Society for Epilepsy
Chalfont Society for Epilepsy
Chalfont St Peter
Buckinghamshire SL9 0RJ
01494 873 991
<www.epilepsynse.org.uk>

Barnardo's
(Can provide counselling or a 'befriending service' for the pupil)
020 8550 8822
<www.barnardos.org.uk>

Physically Disabled and Able Bodied (PHAB)
Summit House, 50 Wandle Road
Croydon CR0 1DF
020 8667 9443

Institute for Sport and Recreational Management (ISRM)
Giffard House, 36/38 Sherrard Street
Melton Mowbray LE13 1XJ
01664 565 531

Appendix 1

Management issues

These are whole school issues to be considered by the Senior Management Team when planning to meet the needs of a pupil with epilepsy.

Consideration:	✔	✘	Action required:
Are the governors aware of their responsibilities in ensuring that the needs of pupils with epilepsy are met?			
Are all staff aware of the educational implications of epilepsy?			
Is there a need for additional adult support for the pupil?			
Are staff appropriately trained?			
Is there effective communication between home and school in place?			
Are other agencies involved in meeting the needs of the pupil?			
Do you know where to seek further information and advice?			
Are you aware of recent legislation, LEA/SEN policies?			
Are there strategies to support the child's emotional well-being?			
Are there strategies to promote positive peer group relationships?			
Do you promote positive images of the child?			
Are appropriate teaching strategies in place?			
Are any additional resources required to support curriculum delivery?			

Commonly used anti-convulsants and possible side effects

First Line Therapy

Drug and uses:	Possible side effects:	Comments:
Lamotrogine (Lamictal) • partial seizures • generalised seizures • absences • tonic-clonic seizures • therapy resultant Lennox-Gastaut Syndrome	• headache • nausea/vomiting • dizziness • ataxia (problems with coordination) • skin rash	*does not make any seizure worse Interacts with: 1. Carbamazepine (Tegretol) 2. Sodium Valproate (Epilim)
Sodium Valproate (Epilim) • partial seizures • generalised seizures • absence seizures • tonic-clonic seizures • juvenile myoclonic epilepsy	• nausea/vomiting • sedation • hair loss • weight gain • tremor	*does not make any seizure worse *can cause defects in foetal development resulting in Sodium Valproate Syndrome
Carbamazepine (Tegretol) • generalised seizures • tonic-clonic seizures • partial focal seizures • complex partial seizures	• sedation • blurred vision • poor balance • Teratagenic affects increase risk of spina bifida	*not to be given in: 1. absence seizures 2. myoclonic seizures 3. juvenile myoclonic seizures
Topiramate (Topamax) • partial facial seizures • generalised seizures • Lennox-Gastaut Syndrome • tonic-clonic seizures	• nausea/vomiting • mild tremor • concentration difficulties • weight loss	*does not make any seizure worse

Second Line Therapy

Drug and uses:	Possible side effects:	Comments:
Phenytoin (Epilim) • partial seizures • complex partial seizures • tonic-clonic seizures	• vertigo • ataxia • headache • sedation	*does not make any seizure worse
Vigabatrin (Sabril) • primary generalised seizures • complex partial seizures • febrile convulsions	• visual field problems • sedation • behavioural problems	Long term usage: • acne like rash • gum hyperplasia • peripheral neuropathy
Gabapentin (Neurontin) • generalised seizures • partial seizures	• dizziness • ataxia	*does not make any seizure worse
Levetiracetam *not licensed for use for those under 16 years of age • partial seizures with or without secondary generalisation	• dizziness • low mood	*does not make any seizure worse

Legal framework for meeting the needs of pupils with epilepsy

The **Department of Health Circular 14/96 'Supporting Pupils with Medical Needs in Schools'** says that:

> 'LEAs, schools and governing bodies are responsible for the health and safety of all pupils in their care'.

Guidance is given based on various documents and the relevant points outlined below.

The **Health and Safety at Work (HSAW) Act 1974** states that employers have a duty towards *employees*. They must:

- prepare a written Health & Safety management policy;
- make sure all staff are aware of the contents of the policy;
- ensure that appropriate safety measures are in place;
- ensure that staff are properly trained.

In their responsibility to *pupils* they must:

- ensure that safety measures cover the needs of all pupils in school, i.e. make special arrangements for specific pupils if required.

Further **The Management of HSAW Regulations 1992** emphasises the need to make 'risk assessments' for all activities and to:

- plan strategies to meet these risks;
- ensure that all staff are aware of these strategies.

If the pupil also has learning difficulties the **Education Act 1996** requires schools and LEAs to meet these special educational needs.

Whether the school initiates an assessment of special educational needs would be judged on an individual basis depending on the severity of the condition and its impact on access to the curriculum and the learning process (see **Code of Practice**). **N.B.** Parental rights have been strengthened by the new CoP (2001) with regard to statementing and can appeal against decisions by both the school and the LEA through the SEN Tribunal.

In Section 322 of this Act it states that the Health Authority is responsible for providing support and advice, e.g. training staff in special procedures to meet a pupil's needs. It also recommends that Health Authorities and schools should work together.

The **Medicines Act 1968** says that:

- there is no legal or contractual duty on school staff to give medication – it is a voluntary role only;

- employers should ensure that insurance policies cover those staff willing to support pupils with medical needs;

- teachers and school staff have a common law duty to act as any parent would ('in loco parentis') to ensure safety.

N.B. This means that they might be required to give medication under exceptional circumstances, e.g. residential visits, school outings, etc. The **Children's Act 1989** covers teachers in these situations.

The **Education (School Premises) Regulations 1996** require schools to provide accommodation to:

- give medical and dental treatment, and care for pupils during school hours (this may not be its sole use).

Also they must ensure:

- safe storage and handling of medicines;

- that medication required in emergency situations is not locked away;

- relevant staff know the location of medicines.

The **DHC 14/96 document** further states that:

- no pupil can be excluded from a school for medical reasons (now strengthened by the Disability Rights Bill 2001);

- the school should write a policy to meet individual pupils' medical needs;

- advice should be sought from the local Health Authority regarding health issues;

- the school should write an Individual Health Care Plan in conjunction with parents and health care professionals to ensure the pupil is supported effectively.

Lastly the **DfES 'SEN and Disability Rights in Education' Bill 2001** says that:

- LEAs and schools have a *joint* responsibility to meet the needs of pupils with special needs;

- these needs must be taken into consideration and planned for well in advance, e.g. timetabling pupils for the ground floor if there are safety issues with stairs;

- schools should provide **equivalent provision** on the ground floor if necessary (to provide **equality of provision**), e.g. if subject provision or SEN base is on the first floor or above;

- if buildings are being modified or a new build planned the special needs of pupils must be borne in mind.

A Whole School Policy

Recognising the individual needs of the pupil with epilepsy

This school will encourage and help pupils with epilepsy to participate fully in the curriculum and all aspects of school life.

This school recognises and understands that epilepsy is a neurological condition affecting as many as 1 in 100 school children.

Staff in **this school** have been trained in the procedure of seizure response should it be required.

This school will ensure that pupils as well as staff understand epilepsy, endeavour to raise awareness of the condition and alleviate the stigma and fear associated with it.

This school acknowledges within its admission procedure that epilepsy is a recognised medical condition and encourages disclosure by parents.

All school personnel need to be aware of the needs of individual pupils with epilepsy – this will include:

- the type and frequency of seizures;
- action required when a seizure occurs;
- medication and possible side effects;
- any known triggers to a seizure;
- the importance of recording seizures occurring, mood changes, etc. to provide an accurate medical history for hospital appointments;
- any safety procedure required in individual subjects, e.g. Food technology, Science, etc.;
- what additional resources are required to support the pupil with epilepsy.

Staff INSET: supporting pupils with epilepsy in mainstream schools

Aims:

- To raise awareness of epilepsy
- To plan to meet the needs of pupils with epilepsy
- To encourage an interdisciplinary approach to supporting pupils
- To allay fears and misunderstandings about epilepsy
- To put recommendations into context for this school

1. Raising awareness of epilepsy

- What is epilepsy?
- Types of epilepsy
- Treatment of epilepsy
- How to respond to a generalised tonic-clonic seizure

2. Planning to meet the needs of pupils with epilepsy

- Whole School Policy
- Nominating staff to administer drugs
- Identifying area for storing/administering drugs
- Record keeping
- Information sharing
- IHCPs – educational implications, side effects of drugs, etc.

3. Encouraging an interdisciplinary approach to supporting pupils with epilepsy

- Home/School/Health liaison

4. Allaying fears and misunderstandings about epilepsy

- What to do when seizures occur – refer to IHCP
- Recognising an emergency – refer to IHCP/school policy
- Triggers, activities to avoid, etc.

5. Putting recommendations into context for this school

- Accurate record and description of pupil's seizures in school/at home
- Importance of forward planning for subjects, physical activities, visits (day and residential), etc.

Tonic-clonic seizure response

Staff should have regular training in the appropriate response to a tonic-clonic seizure which is as follows:

1. Arrange for the other pupils to quietly leave the classroom.
2. Ensure safety by clearing the area around the pupil.*
3. Place something soft under the pupil's head, e.g. a cushion or coat.
4. Loosen the collar and any tight clothing.
5. Do *not* forcibly restrain the pupil unless he/she is in danger.
6. When the seizure has ended put the pupil into the recovery position to maintain a clear airway.

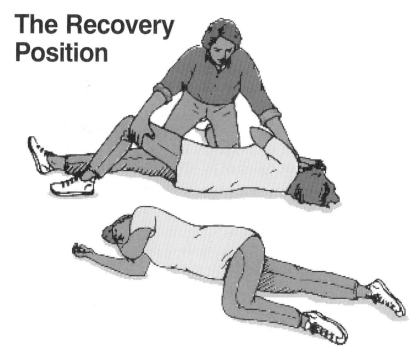

The Recovery Position

7. Stay with the pupil until you are certain recovery is complete. **N.B.** If the seizure lasts more than 5 minutes, or 2 minutes longer than is usual for that pupil, call an ambulance and administer emergency treatment according to the IHCP.
8. Reassure and re-orientate the pupil; explain that he/she has had a seizure and that he/she is safe.
9. Refer to the IHCP for ongoing care, e.g. go home to sleep.
10. Record the seizure and ensure parents have a copy; this can aid diagnosis when the pupil visits the consultant.

*A pupil in a wheelchair should be left in his/her chair until the seizure is over; the head should be supported to ensure the airway is clear. Once the seizure has passed, the pupil can be taken out of the wheelchair and allowed to rest if necessary.

Parental questionnaire

Name:.. DoB: ....

What type of seizure/s does your child have?

....
....
....

How long do they last?

....

What first aid is appropriate?

....
....
....

How long a rest will your child need following a seizure?

....

Are there any conditions that you have noted that might trigger a seizure?

....
....

How often does your child take medication?

....

What is the medication and dosage?

....

Does your child have any warning before a seizure occurs?

....

Are there any activities which the doctor feels may require particular precautions?

....

Does your child have any other medical conditions?

....

Any other relevant information

....

Record of seizures occurring during the school day

Name:.. DoB: ....

Address:...

.... Tel.: ....

Emergency contact numbers: ....

Date of seizure: .... Time it occurred: ....

How long did the seizure last? ....

Action taken (if any): ....

Were there any warning signs? (e.g. mood change, restlessness, sensation, taste, sound, etc.) Ask the pupil to assist in answering the question if appropriate:

....

....

What was he/she doing when the seizure occurred? ....

....

....

Did he/she fall? If so describe: ....

Did he/she lose consciousness? ....

What colour was his/her face? ....

Did his/her body move during the seizure? ....

If so please describe:...

Was there incontinence?   Yes   No   (please ring)

                                 Bladder   Bowel   (please ring)

What was he/she like after the seizure?

Immediate recovery   sleepy   confused   agitated   (please ring)

Other: ....

Was he/she injured during the seizure? ....

Name:.. Post in school:..................................

Date:...

Appendix 9

Individual Health Care Plan for pupils with epilepsy

Name: .... DoB: ....

School: ....

.... Headteacher: ....

Parental contact no.: ....

Type of seizure/s experienced: ....

Symptoms: ....

....

Possible triggers: ....

Usual procedure following seizures: ....

Prescribed anti-epileptic medication: ....

Where medication is stored: ....

Member of staff responsible for replenishment of medication:..........................

Staff trained to give medication: ....

....

For further training contact: ....

.... Tel: ....

Member of staff responsible for Home/School/Health liaison: ....

Emergency procedure if seizure lasts more than .... minutes:

1. Member of staff to stay with… to ensure safety.

2. Quietly clear the classroom of pupils.

3. Inform Headteacher and telephone parents.

4. Telephone 999, ask for Ambulance Service, give name of pupil, address and phone number of school.

5. Trained member of staff to administer rectal diazepam with same sex witness present if possible.

6. Stay with .... until the ambulance arrives.

7. If parents have not arrived by this time a member of staff will accompany to the .... hospital in the ambulance.

8. Fill in seizure record form for the pupil and send a copy to the parents/GP.

Useful addresses and telephone numbers of professionals involved with
....

Service	Name	Address & Tel. no.
Emergency Contact		
Consultant		
Family GP		
Epilepsy/Paediatric/ Community Support Nurse		
Specialist Physician		
Other, e.g. Local Support Group		

Parental Consent Form

I give consent for .... to be given rectal diazepam (Valium/Stesolid) by a trained member of staff in the circumstances described in this document.

I will undertake to inform the school of any changes in the nature of his/her seizures or medication.

Signed: .... Date: ....

Please print name: ....

Appendix 10

Professionals who may be involved with pupils with epilepsy

	Personnel	Telephone number
Special Needs Adviser		
Educational Psychologist		
Physical Disability Service		
SENSS		
Visually Impaired Service		
Hearing Impaired Service		
SENCO		
Education Welfare Officer		
School Nurse		
Epilepsy Support Nurse		
Asthma Support Nurse		
Physiotherapist		
Occupational Therapist		
Speech and Language Therapist		
Social Worker		
Wheelchair Services		

Materials to support PHSE

Primary phase

Projects:

1. Epilepsy is one of the oldest disorders known to man. What books about epilepsy can you find in your local library? Are there any reference books at school to help you?

2. What can you discover about the history of epilepsy?

3. Many famous people have had epilepsy; can you find out more about them? Who are they and what have they achieved?

4. EEG is short for electroencephalogram, a test carried out on most people being investigated for epilepsy. Can you find out more about it? How is it carried out and what sort of results are obtained?

Secondary phase

Discussion points:

'Most people, including employers, tend to react to epilepsy with a mixture of alarm and uncertainty about how far someone with epilepsy can lead a normal working life.'

Based on your findings do you think their fears are justified?

'There are many famous people with epilepsy and the condition did not seem to stop them from succeeding.'

Knowing this do you think it would help the ordinary person with epilepsy?

'To a great extent, the social problems of people with epilepsy are created by the attitude of society towards them.'

Discuss…

'People with epilepsy can themselves often be very influential in shaping the attitudes of those around them.'

What information can those with epilepsy provide, that would influence people, and how do you think they could pass this on to the general public?

Adapted from 'Pupil Materials' provided by Epilepsy Action

Glossary

Abbreviations used:

SCMO	Schools Clinical Medical Officer
CSA	Child Support Assistant
IEP	Individual Education Plan
IHCP	Individual Health Care Plan
INSET	In-service Training
SENCO	Special Educational Needs Coordinator
NSE	National Society for Epilepsy

Improve your support for pupils with SEN with other books in this series...

The books in this series gather together all the vital knowledge and practical support that schools need to meet specific special needs. Information is simply explained and clearly sign-posted so that practitioners can quickly access what they need to know. Each book describes a specific area of special educational need and explains how it might present difficulties for pupils within the school setting. Checklists and photocopiable forms are provided to help save time and develop good practice.

Supporting Children with Behaviour Difficulties
£10.00 • Paperback • 64 A4 pages • 1-84312-228-6 • July 2004

Supporting Children with Motor Co-ordination Difficulties
£10.00 • Paperback • 64 A4 pages • 1-84312-227-8 • July 2004

Supporting Children with Fragile X Syndrome
£10.00 • Paperback • 64 A4 pages • 1-84312-226-X • July 2004

Supporting Children with Speech and Language Difficulties
£10.00 • Paperback • 144 A4 pages • 1-84312-225-1 • July 2004

Supporting Children with Medical Conditions
£20.00 • Paperback • 144 A4 pages • 1-84312-224-3 • May 2004

Supporting Children with Epilepsy
£10.00 • Paperback • 64 A4 pages • 1-84312-223-5 • May 2004

Supporting Children with Dyslexia
£10.00 • Paperback • 48 A4 pages • 1-84312-222-7 • July 2004

Supporting Children with Down's Syndrome
£10.00 • Paperback • 48 A4 pages • 1-84312-221-9 • May 2004

Supporting Children with Cerebral Palsy
£10.00 • Paperback • 48 A4 pages • 1-84312-220-0 • May 2004

Supporting Children with Autistic Spectrum Disorder
£10.00 • Paperback • 64 A4 pages • 1-84312-219-7 • May 2004

Supporting Children with Asthma
£10.00 • Paperback • 48 A4 pages • 1-84312-218-9 • May 2004

ORDER FORM

Qty	ISBN	Title	Price	Subtotal
	1-84312-218-9	Supporting Children with Asthma	£10.00	
	1-84312-219-7	Supporting Children with ASD	£10.00	
	1-84312-228-6	Supporting Children with Behaviour Ds	£10.00	
	1-84312-220-0	Supporting Children with Cerebral Palsy	£10.00	
	1-84312-221-9	Supporting Children with Down's Syndrome	£10.00	
	1-84312-222-7	Supporting Children with Dyslexia	£10.00	
	1-84312-223-5	Supporting Children with Epilepsy	£10.00	
	1-84312-226-X	Supporting Children with Fragile X Syndrome	£10.00	
	1-84312-224-3	Supporting Children with Medical Conditions	£20.00	
	1-84312-227-8	Supporting Children with MCDs	£10.00	
	1-84312-225-1	Supporting Children with S&L Difficulties	£10.00	
	1-84312-204-9	David Fulton Catalogue	FREE	

Postage and Packing: FREE to schools, LEAs and other institutions.
£2.50 per order for private/personal orders.
Prices and publication dates are subject to change.

| P&P | |
| TOTAL | |

Please complete delivery details:

Name: ....

Organisation: ....

....

Address: ....

....

....

....

Postcode: ....

Tel: ....

Email: ....

☐ Please add me to your email mailing list

Send your order to our distributors:

**HarperCollins Publishers
Customer Service Centre
Westerhill Road • Bishopbriggs
Glasgow • G64 2QT**

Tel. 0870 787 1721

Fax. 0870 787 1723

or order online at
www.fultonpublishers.co.uk

Payment:
☐ Please invoice (applicable to schools, LEAs and other institutions)
☐ I enclose a cheque payable to David Fulton Publishers Ltd (include postage and packing if applicable)
☐ Please charge to my credit card (Visa/Barclaycard, Access/Mastercard, American Express, Switch, Delta)

card number

expiry date

(Switch customers only) valid from   issue number